SOCCER HOT STREAKS

BY EMMA HUDDLESTON

MOMENTUM

Published by The Child's World®
1980 Lookout Drive • Mankato, MN 56003-1705
800-599-READ • www.childsworld.com

Photographs ©: Mo Khursheed/TFV Media/AP
Images, cover, 1, 18; Alizada Studios/Shutterstock
Images, 5; Jed Leicester/Reuters/Newscom,
6; Alastair Grant/AP Images, 9; Luca Bruno/AP
Images, 10; Dick Druckman/AP Images, 13; Alicia
Chelini/Shutterstock Images, 14; Themba Hadebe/
AP Images, 16; Darryl Dyck/The Canadian Press/
AP Images, 21; Elaine Thompson/AP Images,
22; Red Line Editorial, 23; Oleksandr Osipov/
Shutterstock Images, 24, 27, 28

ISBN 9781503832343
LCCN 2018963097

Printed in the United States of America
PA02422

ABOUT THE AUTHOR

Emma Huddleston lives in Minnesota with her husband. She enjoys writing
children's books, but she likes reading novels even more. When she is not writing
or reading, she likes to stay active by running, hiking, or swing dancing.

CONTENTS

MOMENTUM

FAST FACTS

Soccer Is Born

▶ Soccer is called football in many countries.

▶ The first soccer organization was formed in England in 1863. It is known as the Football Association.

▶ In 1862, the first organized soccer club was formed in the United States. The Oneidas played in Boston, Massachusetts. Today, a monument marks the place where the team played home games.

First World Cup

▶ The World Cup for men occurs every four years. Thirty-two teams from all around the world take part in this soccer competition.

▶ The first World Cup was held in 1930 in Uruguay. The host country won the first championship.

▶ The first Women's World Cup was in 1991 in China. The United States won. Like the men's World Cup, the tournament takes place every four years.

**Soccer games have two 45-minute halves. ▶
The total game time is 90 minutes.**

CHAPTER ONE

ARSENAL'S UNDEFEATED SEASON

When Thierry Henry walked out onto the field, he heard the crowd cheer for the seemingly invincible team. Going into the final game of the 2003–04 season, Arsenal had still not lost. It had been more than 100 years since a team went undefeated in England's first division. People called Arsenal "the Invincibles."[1] But first, Henry and Arsenal had to get past Leicester City.

The sun shined down on Arsenal's home stadium. Fans danced and cheered. Henry, a star **forward**, took a deep breath and waited for the referee's whistle. When the game started, Leicester played hard. Henry and his teammates couldn't break through the Leicester defense. Then disaster struck. Leicester's Paul Dickov got open in front of Arsenal's goal. A teammate passed him the ball, and he headed it into the net. Suddenly, Arsenal's streak was in trouble.

◀ **Thierry Henry scored 29 goals going into the game against Leicester City.**

Henry wasn't worried. He knew Arsenal had come from behind to win just one month earlier against Liverpool. The team only needed to find an opportunity. After halftime, that opportunity came. Arsenal defender Ashley Cole had the ball. A Leicester defender took him down. Because the play was in the penalty box, the referee called for a penalty kick. Henry stepped up to take it.

Henry lined up several steps behind the ball. His socks were pulled up high. His eyes were focused on the goal. When the referee blew his whistle, Henry raced forward. On his sixth step, Henry swung through the ball with his right foot. The ball struck off the inside of his foot and sailed into the bottom left corner of the goal. Arsenal had tied the game. "The record is still in sight!" yelled the announcer.[2]

The team wanted more than a tie, though. Around 20 minutes later, Arsenal captain Patrick Vieira scored again. When the final whistle blew, Arsenal had won 2–1. Henry, Vieira, and their teammates met on the field. They locked arms, made a circle, and jumped in celebration. Arsenal was officially invincible.

Henry started playing for Arsenal in 1999. ▶

CHAPTER TWO

HOPE SOLO'S SHUTOUT SKILLS

Hope Solo put on her **goalkeeper** gloves in the locker room. The fabric felt familiar as she tightened the gloves on her wrists. It was the 2008 Olympics final in Beijing, China. Solo had started in every game in the Olympics so far. In this game, the United States would play Brazil. Brazil had a strong offense. Solo knew it would be a tough competition.

When she walked onto the field, the crowd was already cheering. Fans from around the world were watching. In the first half, no one scored. The scoreboard still read 0–0 in the second half when Solo saw an **opponent** dribbling down the field. Brazil was trying to score. The player dribbled around the U.S. defenders. Then she took a big step and shot the ball. It was up to Solo to protect the goal.

◄ **Hope Solo celebrates her team's accomplishments at the 2008 Olympics.**

Solo was ready. She had her knees bent and her eyes locked on the ball. Her hands were out to the sides, and she wiggled her fingers. Once the ball started flying through the air, Solo had to react quickly. She reached her arm out to the side and knocked the ball down. It landed on the ground in front of the net. One of her teammates kicked the ball farther away from the goal. The save maintained the **shutout**. When one of Solo's teammates scored a goal in **extra time**, the United States won 1–0.

Solo was one of the most skilled goalkeepers of all time. Her skills helped her get a lot of shutouts. In the 2015 Women's World Cup, Solo did not allow any goals in five games. With ten career shutouts in Women's World Cup play, Solo also tied a tournament record.

FROM FORWARD TO GOALKEEPER

When Solo was young, she was a talented forward. She liked running down the field and scoring goals. But one day, when she was 15 years old, her team's regular goalkeeper got injured. Solo had to take her place. She didn't really like playing goalkeeper. It wasn't until college that she decided to play the position full-time. By then she loved being a goalkeeper. She was successful at it, too.

▲ **Solo (in green) leaps into the air to stop a shot by Brazil in the final Olympic soccer game. The U.S. team won a gold medal.**

Then Solo passed another milestone in July 2016. The U.S. Women's National Team played South Africa in Chicago. Solo was in goal. She watched the ball fly through the air toward the goal. A South Africa player kicked it to a teammate, who **deflected** it toward the goal. Solo was waiting and safely picked it up. That was as close as South Africa would come to scoring.

The United States won the game 1–0, and Solo became the first goalkeeper in the world to pass the 100-shutout milestone. She ended her career with 102 shutouts. She still holds the world record for most career shutouts. When she reflected on her career, she said, "I couldn't have been a great goalkeeper without power, agility and quickness."[3]

CHAPTER THREE

TIM HOWARD'S 16 SAVES

Goalkeeper Tim Howard's toe barely hit the ball, knocking it out of bounds. It was a close save. The 2014 World Cup game against Belgium was less than one minute old. Already the talented Belgian team was attacking hard. Howard and his U.S. teammates would need to play their best to stop them. After all, with a loss they'd be eliminated.

A Belgian player dribbled around a U.S. defender. He was far from the goal. He took a big step to prepare for a shot. Howard had his eyes on the ball. Once the Belgian player kicked the ball, Howard dove onto it. That was Howard's fifth save of the game. He was on a hot streak. Not long after that, Howard was tested again. A Belgian player was dribbling quickly down the field. Howard took a few steps forward in front of the goal. The Belgian player passed the ball through the air to his teammate.

◄ **Tim Howard has played for various soccer clubs, including Everton and Manchester United in England.**

▲ **Many people were impressed by Howard's amazing saves.**

His teammate jumped and headed the ball. It went flying toward the goal. Howard sprang into the air, reached his arm as high as he could, and tipped the ball over the top of the net.

The crowd cheered for Howard's brilliant play. He continued to make spectacular saves. After his 13th save, Howard did not realize that he had just tied the World Cup record for most saves in one game. But the game was not yet finished.

After 90 minutes of play, the score was tied 0–0, so the game went into extra time. Howard and his team were working hard. Sweat dripped down his face and into his beard, but he wasn't distracted.

Unfortunately for the U.S. team, Howard's heroics couldn't last forever. This time, a Belgian player dribbled up the field and took a close shot. Howard lunged to his right, but the ball was just beyond his reach. It went past the post and into the goal. The U.S. team wasn't done yet. But neither was Belgium. Again, a Belgian player dribbled down the field. Two U.S. defenders tried to stop him. He moved around the defenders and kicked the ball low to the ground. As it came toward the goal, Howard slid and knocked it away with his feet. He made 16 saves in the game.

In the end, Howard's saves were not enough. The final score was 2–1, and Belgium beat the United States. But Howard set a World Cup record for most saves in one game. He said, "We played a great game of football. We left it all out there and we got beat by a really good team."[4]

CHAPTER FOUR

CARLI LLOYD'S HAT TRICK

Players from both teams crowded into the penalty box in front of Japan's goal. Everyone had their eyes on the edge of the field where Megan Rapinoe of the U.S. Women's National Team was preparing to take a corner kick. As soon as her foot made contact with the ball, U.S. forward Carli Lloyd ran quickly toward the goal. The ball bounced across the ground toward the penalty spot, and Lloyd was there to kick it into the net. Less than three minutes had passed in the 2015 Women's World Cup final, and the United States was already leading Japan 1–0.

A few minutes later, Lloyd found herself in a similar situation. She was in a crowd of players near Japan's goal. A teammate sent the ball toward the front of the goal. Japan's defense tried to get control of the ball and kick it away. The players' blue jerseys blocked Lloyd's view. Lloyd saw the ball bounce sideways.

◄ **Carli Lloyd (left) fought to get the ball away from a Japan player during the 2015 Women's World Cup final.**

It was in front of the goal. Lloyd knew this was her chance. She ran at the ball as it moved higher into the air. She jumped and positioned her knee so she could kick it with the inside of her foot. Japan's goalkeeper dove to the right, so Lloyd kicked it in the other direction and scored again. She flexed her arms and yelled in excitement. The game was only five minutes old, and already the United States was up 2–0.

Defenders knew Lloyd was dangerous when she was in front of the goal. But the U.S. midfielder was feeling confident. Lloyd got the ball just shy of midfield. She dribbled past two defenders. Then she noticed Japan's goalkeeper had moved up field. The goalkeeper wasn't expecting any shots while the ball was so far away. Lloyd had other ideas. From the midfield line, she swung her right foot through the ball. Lloyd held her breath as the ball soared through the air. Japan's goalkeeper had no shot. She tried to get back to the goal, but the ball went over her head and in. Lloyd broke into a smile. The crowd went wild. Lloyd had scored a **hat trick** in a Women's World Cup final. And she had done so in just 16 minutes.

The United States won the game with a final score of 5–2. It was the team's third Women's World Cup title. The achievement set a record for the most Women's World Cup wins overall.

In soccer, players are allowed to hit the ▶ ball with their heads. Lloyd (top) did this during the game against Japan.

▲ **U.S. players hold the World Cup trophy up high after winning the game.**

As Lloyd and her teammates raised the golden trophy in the air, they cheered and waved to the crowd. The crowd yelled, jumped, and celebrated, too. Lloyd said, "I want to keep getting better and better. . . . Playing the game I love is joyful. So I keep pushing, keep working."[5]

ALL-TIME WORLD CUP TOP SCORERS AS OF 2018

WOMEN'S SOCCER

NAME	TEAM	GOALS
Marta Vieira de Silva	Brazil	15
Birgit Prinz	Germany	14
Abby Wambach	United States	14
Michelle Akers	United States	12
Sun Wen	China	11
Bettina Wiegmann	Germany	11

MEN'S SOCCER

NAME	TEAM	GOALS
Miroslav Klose	Germany	16
Ronaldo	Brazil	15
Gerd Müller	Germany	14
Just Fontaine	France	13
Pelé	Brazil	12

CHAPTER FIVE

ADA HEGERBERG'S RECORD GOALS

It was time for another corner kick. Ada Hegerberg stood in front of the goal with her teammates from the French team Olympique Lyon in line behind her. They were eager to score. Hegerberg began next to an opponent from the Polish team Medyk Konin. They both breathed heavily. Hegerberg was trying to focus on the play. As soon as she heard the referee's whistle, she turned her head. She saw her teammate kick the ball from the corner. The ball was coming toward her. Hegerberg jumped and headed the ball into the corner of the goal. She had scored her second goal of the game. One of her teammates ran over and gave her a high five. Another teammate hugged her. The 2017–18 European Women's Champions League tournament was only just beginning, and Hegerberg was starting a scoring streak.

◄ **Ada Hegerberg has scored more than 200 goals during her soccer career.**

During the second half against Medyk Konin, Hegerberg ran toward the goal. Her teammate was dribbling quickly down the field. When the teammate passed the ball beyond the line of defense, another Lyon player ran after it. She crossed it to Hegerberg in front of the goal. The goalkeeper started reaching for the ball, but Hegerberg was faster. She kicked it into the net to complete her hat trick. The final score of the game was Olympique Lyon 5, Medyk Konin 0.

After beating Medyk Konin, Lyon kept winning and reached the Women's Champions League final against Wolfsburg, a German team. It was a close game. Neither team scored in the first 90 minutes, so the game went into extra time.

THE SCORERS' LIST

After the 2017–18 season, Hegerberg had scored 37 goals in 37 Women's Champions League matches throughout her career. That puts her in the top ten for the all-time Women's Champions League scorers' list. Hegerberg has a good chance at setting the career record. Going into the 2018–19 season, German star Anja Mittag was on top of the career list with 51 goals.

▲ **Hegerberg fought for control of the ball during the match.**

Wolfsburg scored first, and Hegerberg knew her team needed to work together to win. She wiped the sweat off her forehead and got ready to play. Minutes later, a teammate scored.

▲ **Hegerberg and her teammates were proud of winning the Women's Champions League.**

Hegerberg ran with her arms out to her sides to celebrate. They had tied the game. Then, another teammate scored, and it was 2–1. But the game was not over yet.

A Lyon player was running down the sideline. Hegerberg ran parallel down the center of the field. A defender moved toward one of Hegerberg's teammates, leaving Hegerberg open. She raised her hand to signal her teammate to pass her the ball. Her teammate saw Hegerberg, so she sent the ball soaring toward her. As soon as the ball touched the ground, Hegerberg was there to kick it into the goal. She yelled and pumped her fists in excitement. Olympique Lyon won the Women's Champions League championship against Wolfsburg. The final score was 4–1. With that shot, Hegerberg set the record for most goals scored in a Women's Champions League season with 15. She said, "It is a joy to go to work every day doing what you love the most."[6]

THINK ABOUT IT

► How do teams work together to play soccer? Why do you think it is important for teams to work together?
► How is playing soccer different from playing other sports? How are the rules different? How are they similar?
► Why is playing defense important in soccer? How can the goalkeeper make a difference during the game?

GLOSSARY

deflected (di-FLEKT-ed): Deflected means to change the direction of something. The soccer player deflected the ball toward the goal.

extra time (EK-struh TIME): Extra time is 30 additional minutes added to the regular 90 minutes of a tied soccer game. Howard and the U.S. team played extra time against Belgium in the 2014 World Cup.

forward (FOR-wurd): A forward is a soccer player who focuses on scoring goals and playing offense. Henry is a forward who has scored many goals.

goalkeeper (GOHL-kee-pur): A goalkeeper is one player from each team that is chosen to defend the goal, and he or she can use his or her hands. Howard was the goalkeeper for the U.S. Men's National Team.

hat trick (HAT TRIK): A hat trick is when one player scores three or more goals in a single game. Lloyd scored an impressive hat trick in the 2015 Women's World Cup final.

opponent (uh-POH-nuhnt): An opponent is a player or team you are competing against. Henry dribbled the ball around an opponent to get closer to the goal.

shutout (SHUT-out): A shutout happens when a goalkeeper or team does not let their opponent score. Solo and the U.S. team won a shutout game against Brazil in the 2008 Olympics.

SOURCE NOTES

1. Leo Chan. "'The Invincibles' Arsenal 2003–04 Analysis (1)—Squad and Formation." *Football Performance Analysis.* Football Performance Analysis, 1 Oct. 2013. Web. 15 Nov. 2018.

2. Arsenal Videos. "Round 38: Arsenal 2–1 Leicester City [2003–2004]." *YouTube.* YouTube, 13 July 2017. Web. 15 Nov. 2018.

3. "Hope Solo." *ESPN.* ESPN. 6 Oct. 2011. Web. 15 Nov. 2018.

4. Dan Itel. "World Cup: USMNT Goalkeeper Tim Howard Sets World Cup Record with 16 Saves vs. Belgium." *Major League Soccer.* MLS, 1 July 2014. Web. 15 Nov. 2018.

5. Anthea Levi. "5 Quotes from Carli Lloyd's Memoir That Will Inspire You to Be Your Best." *Health.* Meredith Health Group, 26 Sept. 2016. Web. 15 Nov. 2018.

6. Paul Saffer. "How Brilliant Is Record-Breaker Ada Hegerberg?" *UEFA.* UEFA, 4 June 2018. Web. 15 Nov. 2018.

TO LEARN MORE

BOOKS

Christopher, Matt. *World Cup: An Action-Packed Look at Soccer's Biggest Competition.* New York, NY: Little, Brown and Company, 2018.

Osborne, Mary Pope, and Natalie Pope Boyce. *Soccer.* New York, NY: Random House, 2014.

Zuckerman, Gregory. *Rising Above: How 11 Athletes Overcame Challenges in Their Youth to Become Stars.* New York, NY: Philomel Books, 2016.

WEBSITES

Visit our website for links about soccer: **childsworld.com/links**

Note to Parents, Teachers, and Librarians: We routinely verify our Web links to make sure they are safe and active sites. So encourage your readers to check them out!

INDEX